03	Bewitched	SAMUEL BARNETT & RICHARD SISSON
10	Don't Get Around Much Anymore	ETTA JAMES
14	Embraceable You	JOE WILLIAMS
18	Every Time We Say Goodbye	JULIE LONDON
22	Fly Me To The Moon	DIANA KRALL
26	A Foggy Day	FRANK SINATRA
31	Give Me The Simple Life	JAMIE CULLUM
42	I Get A Kick Out Of You	STEVE TYRELL
36	I Wish I Knew How It Would Feel To Be Free	NINA SIMONE
49	I've Got You Under My Skin	PEGGY LEE
54	The Lady Is A Tramp	ROSEMARY CLOONEY
58	Let There Be Love	NAT 'KING' COLE
63	Mad About The Boy	DINAH WASHINGTON
72	Miss Otis Regrets	CLARE TEAL
68	My Funny Valentine	CHET BAKER
77	'Round Midnight	CARMEN McRAE
86	Strange Fruit	BILLIE HOLIDAY
90	That Old Black Magic	CARMEN McRAE
97	What A Difference A Day Makes	SARAH VAUGHAN
100	Witchcraft	ELLA FITZGERALD

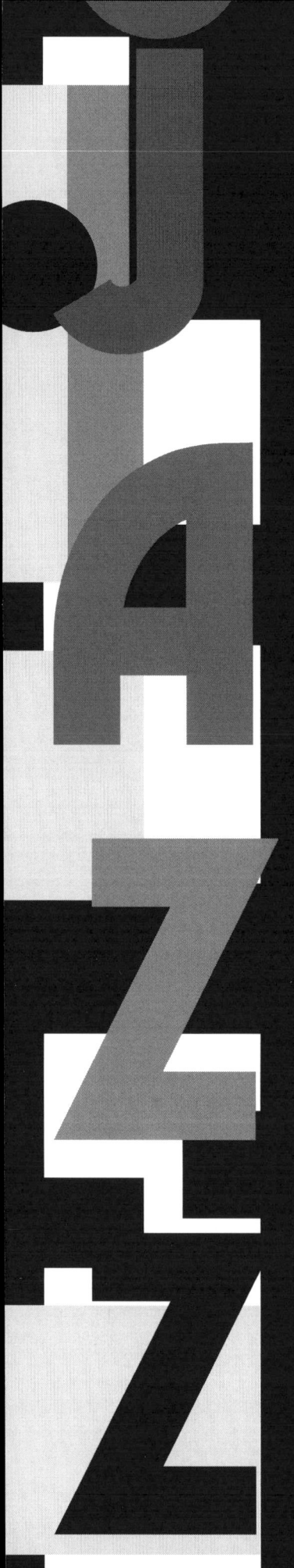

© 2008 by Faber Music Ltd
First published by Faber Music Ltd in 2008
Bloomsbury House
74–77 Great Russell Street
London WC1B 3DA
Arranged by Olly Weeks
Edited by Lucy Holliday
Photographs © Beryl Bryden, Gai Terrell, Herman Leonard,
Bob Willoughby & Redferns Music Picture Libray
Designed by Lydia Merrills-Ashcroft
Printed in England by Caligraving Ltd
All rights reserved

ISBN10: 0-571-53166-0
EAN13: 978-0-571-53166-0

Reproducing this music in any form is illegal and forbidden by
the Copyright, Designs and Patents Act, 1988

To buy Faber Music publications or to find out about the full range of titles available,
please contact your local music retailer or Faber Music sales enquiries:

Faber Music Ltd, Burnt Mill, Elizabeth Way, Harlow, CM20 2HX England
Tel: +44(0)1279 82 89 82   Fax: +44(0)1279 82 89 83
sales@fabermusic.com   fabermusicstore.com

Samuel Barnett & Richard Sisson

BEWITCHED

Words by Lorenz Hart
Music by Richard Rodgers

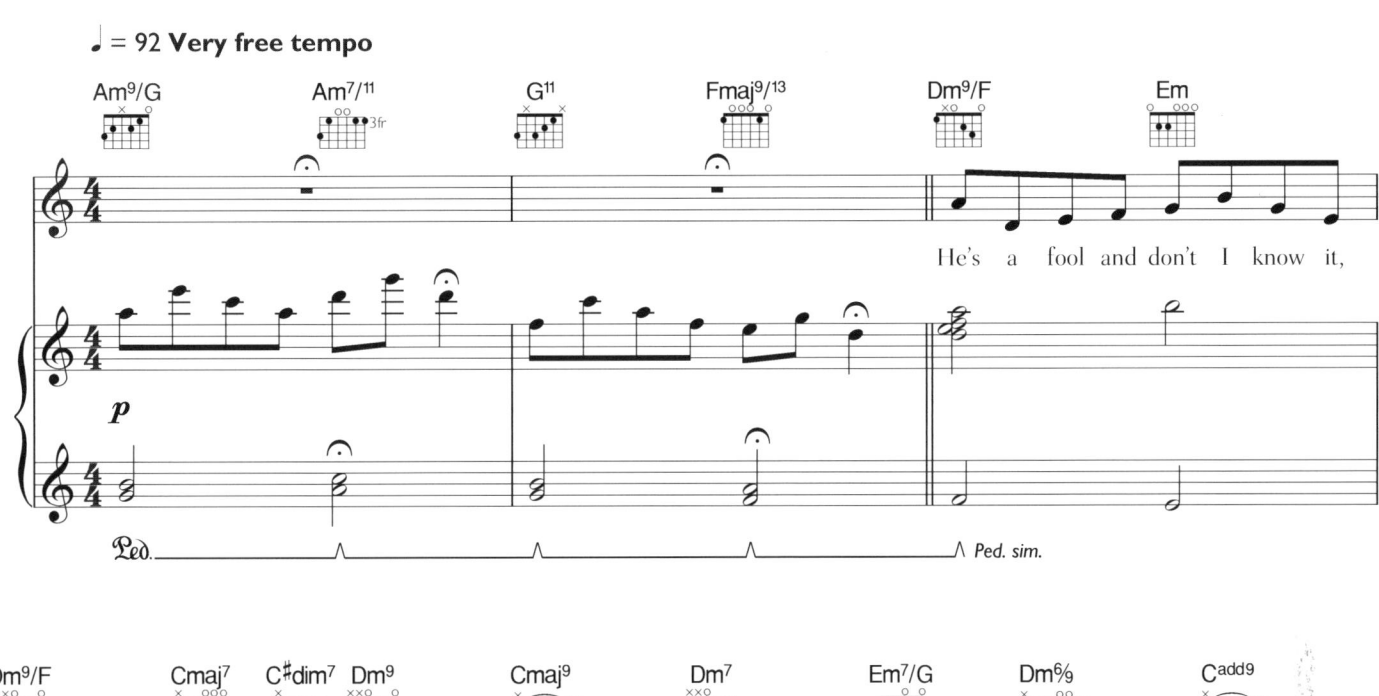

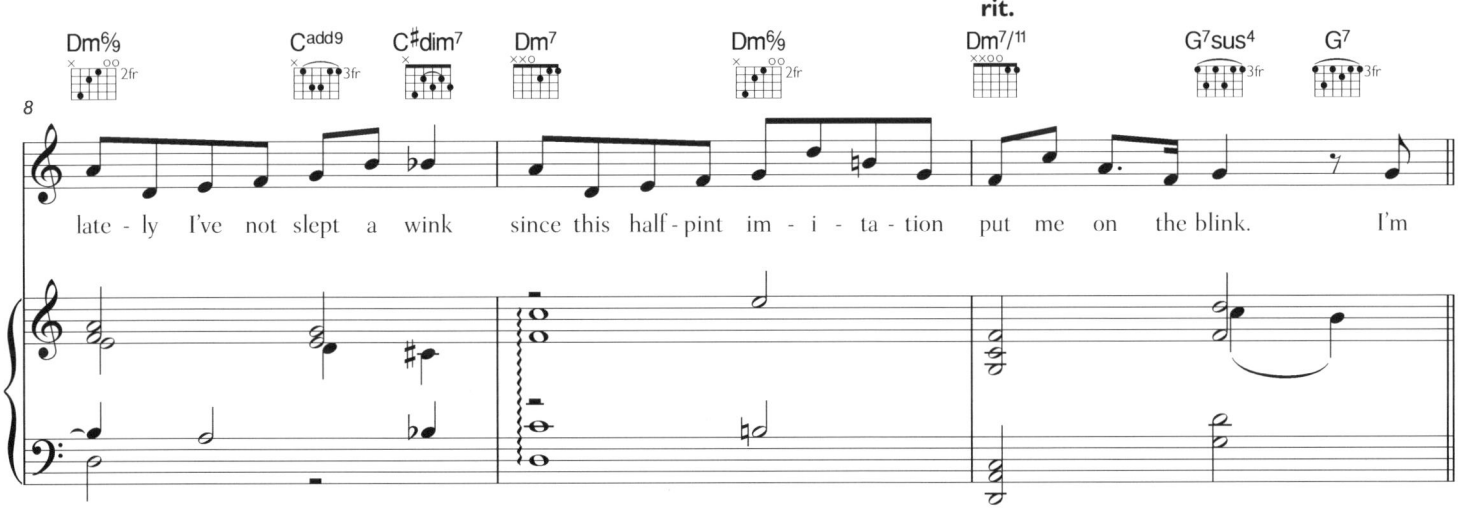

© 1941 Chappell & Co Inc
Warner/Chappell Music Publishing Ltd and
Warner/Chappell North America Ltd

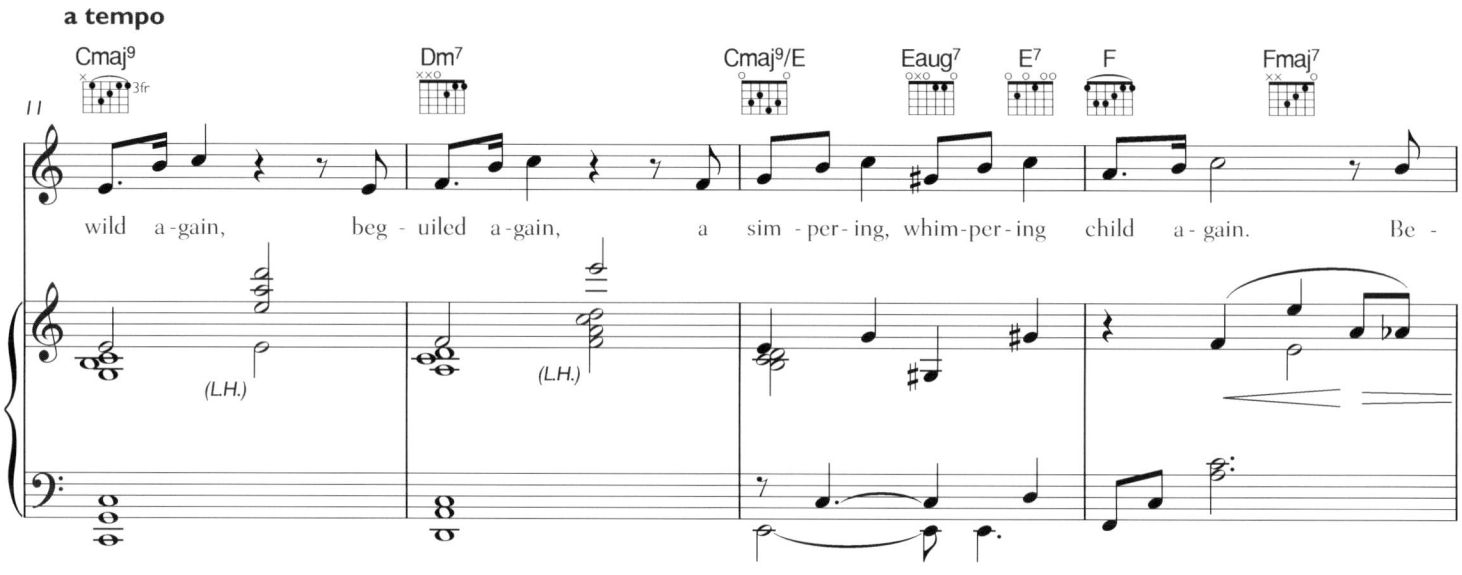
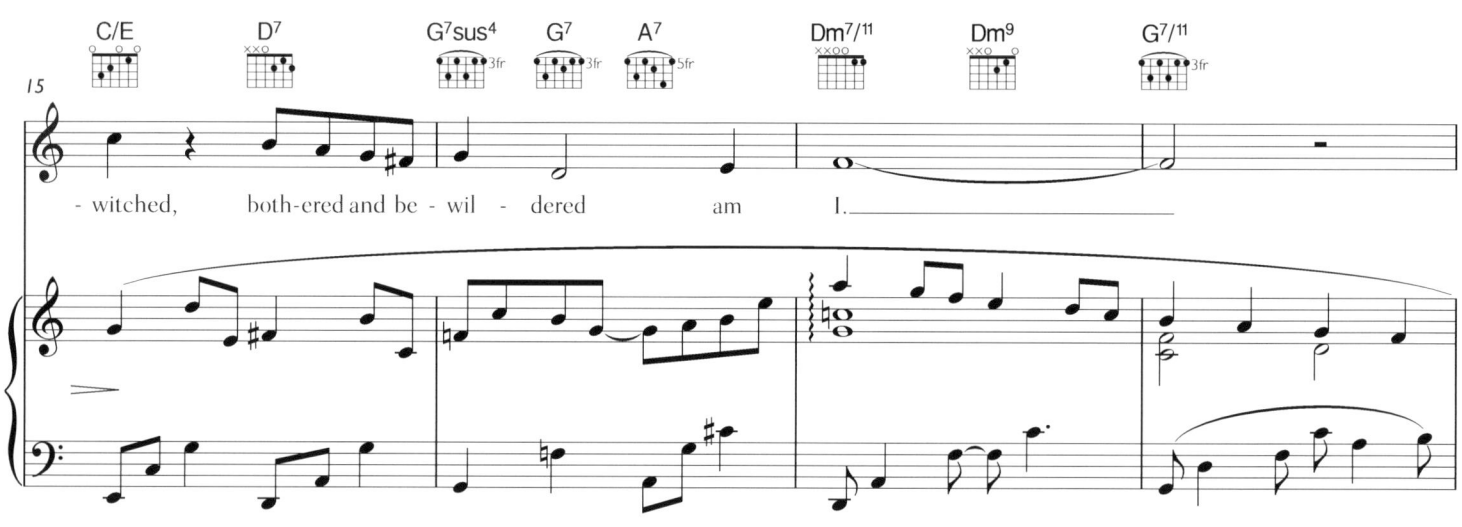
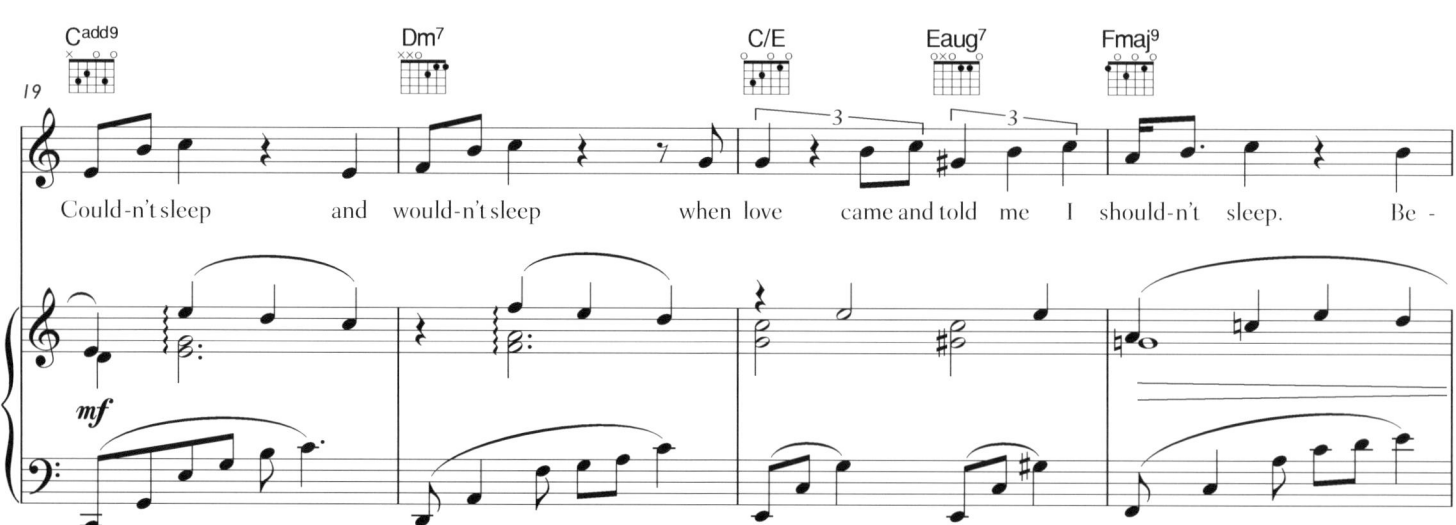

DON'T GET AROUND MUCH ANYMORE

Words by Bob Russell
Music by Duke Ellington

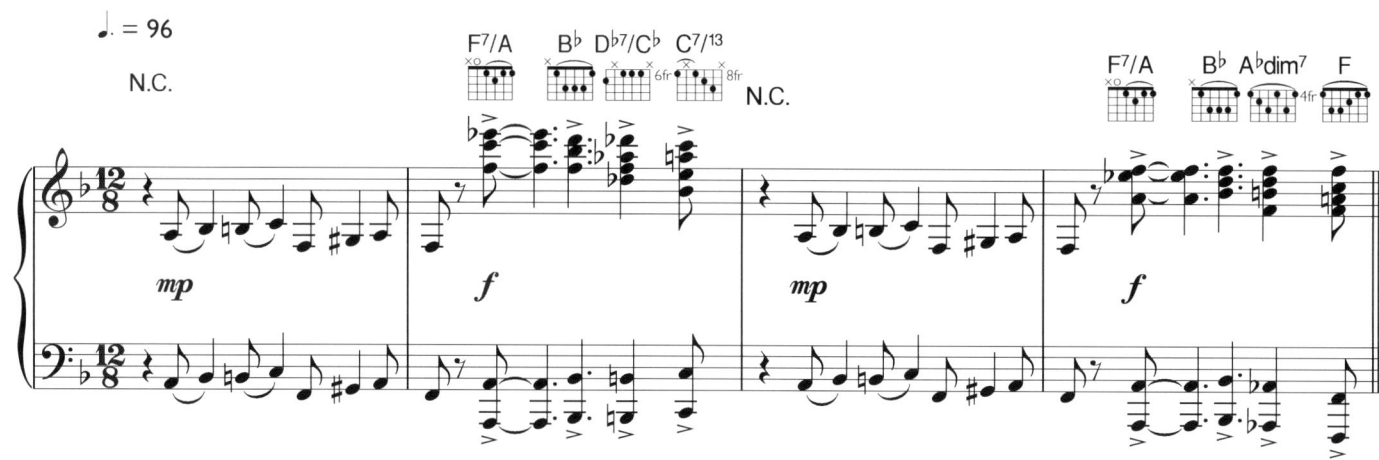

Missed the Sat-ur-day dance, heard they crowd-ed the floor,

could-n't bear it with-out you,

© 1942 Harrison Music Corp and EMI Robbins Catalog Inc
EMI United Partnership Ltd (Publishing), Alfred Publishing Co (Print) and
Chelsea Music Publishing Co Ltd
Print Rights for EMI United Partnership Ltd Administered in Europe by Faber Music Ltd

EMBRACEABLE YOU

Words and Music by George Gershwin and Ira Gershwin

© 1930 Chappell & Co Inc
Warner/Chappell North America Ltd and Ira Gershwin

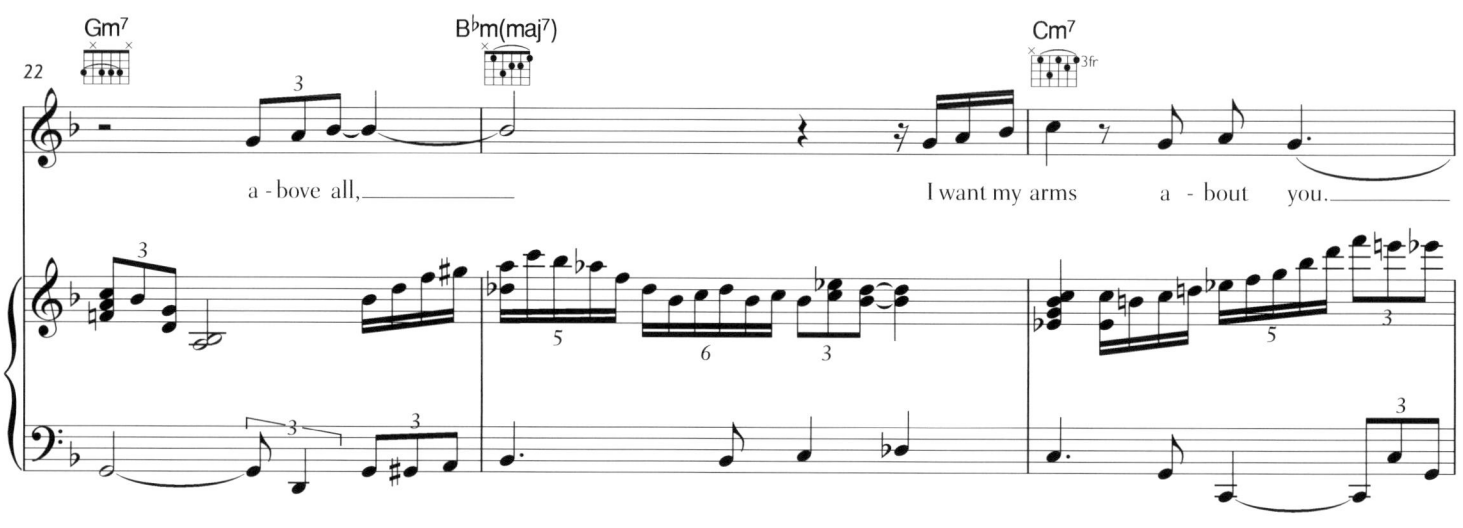
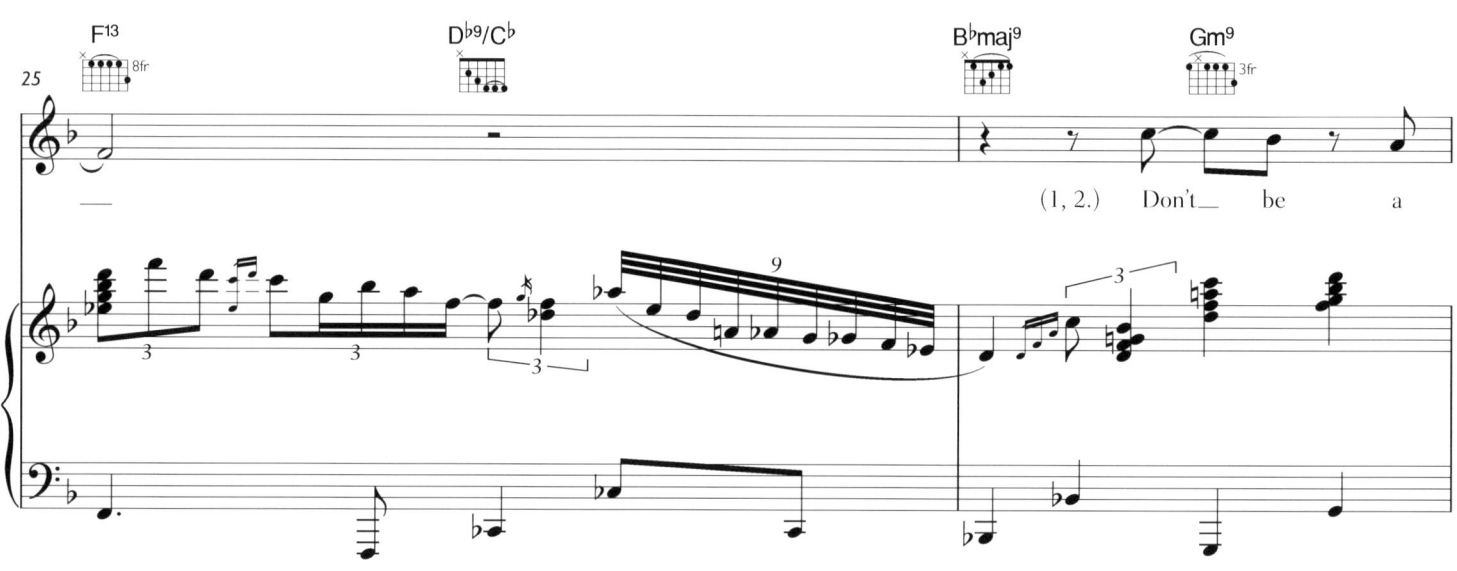

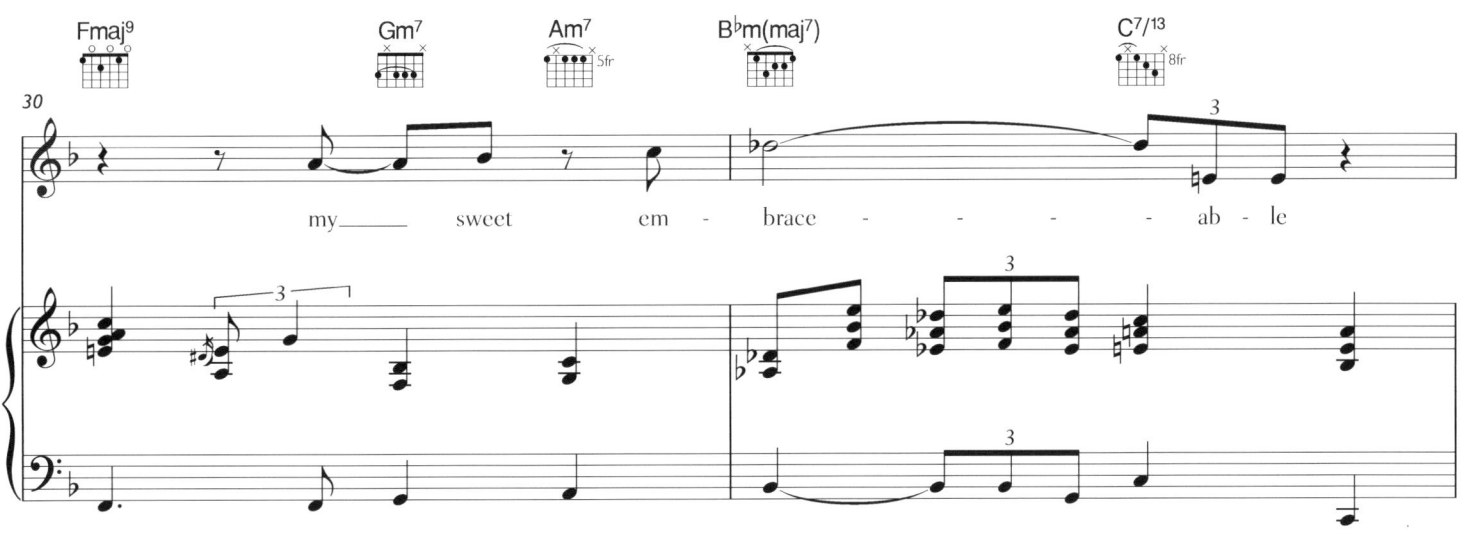

EV'RY TIME WE SAY GOODBYE

Words and Music by Cole Porter

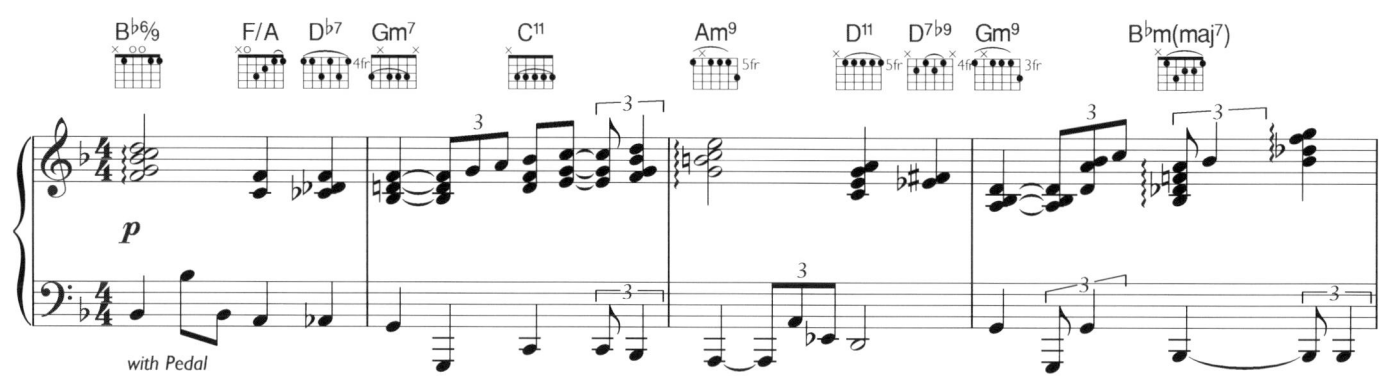

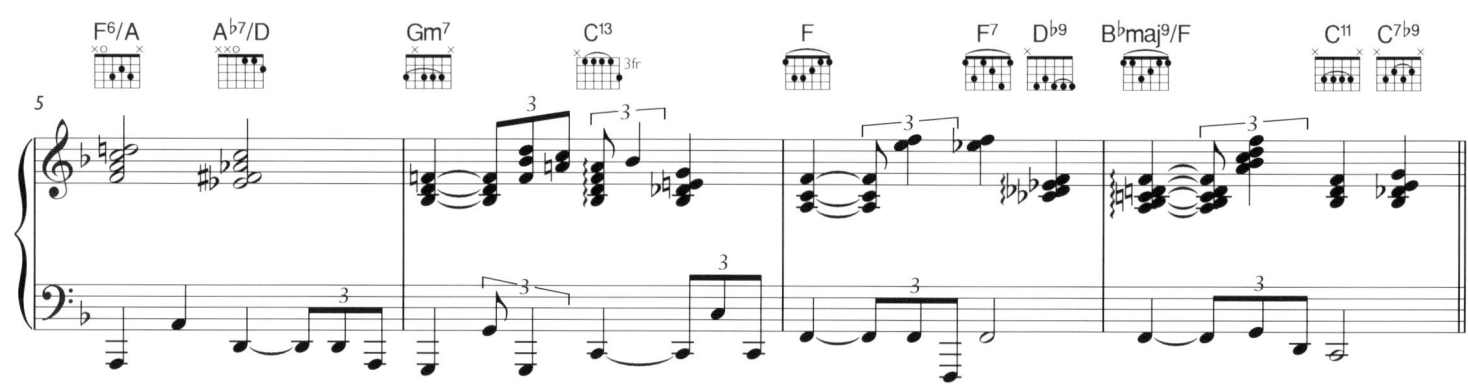

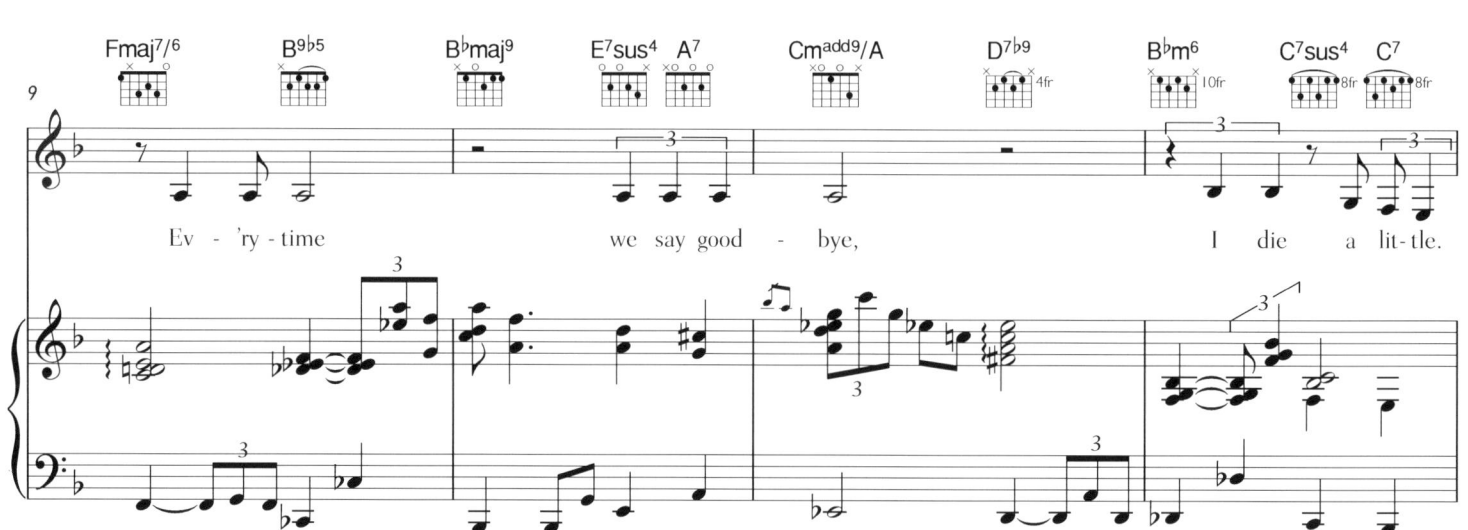

© 1944 Chappell & Co Inc
Warner/Chappell North America Ltd

FLY ME TO THE MOON
(IN OTHER WORDS)

Words and Music by Bart Howard

© 1954 (renewed) Hampshire House Publishing Corp
TRO Essex Music Ltd

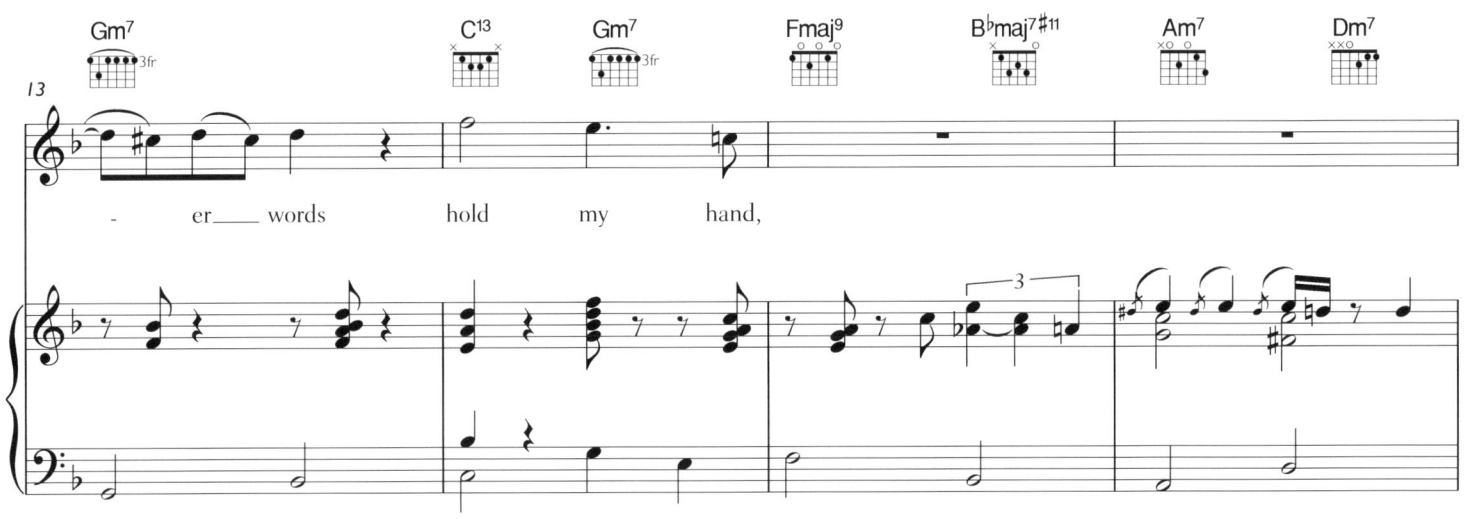

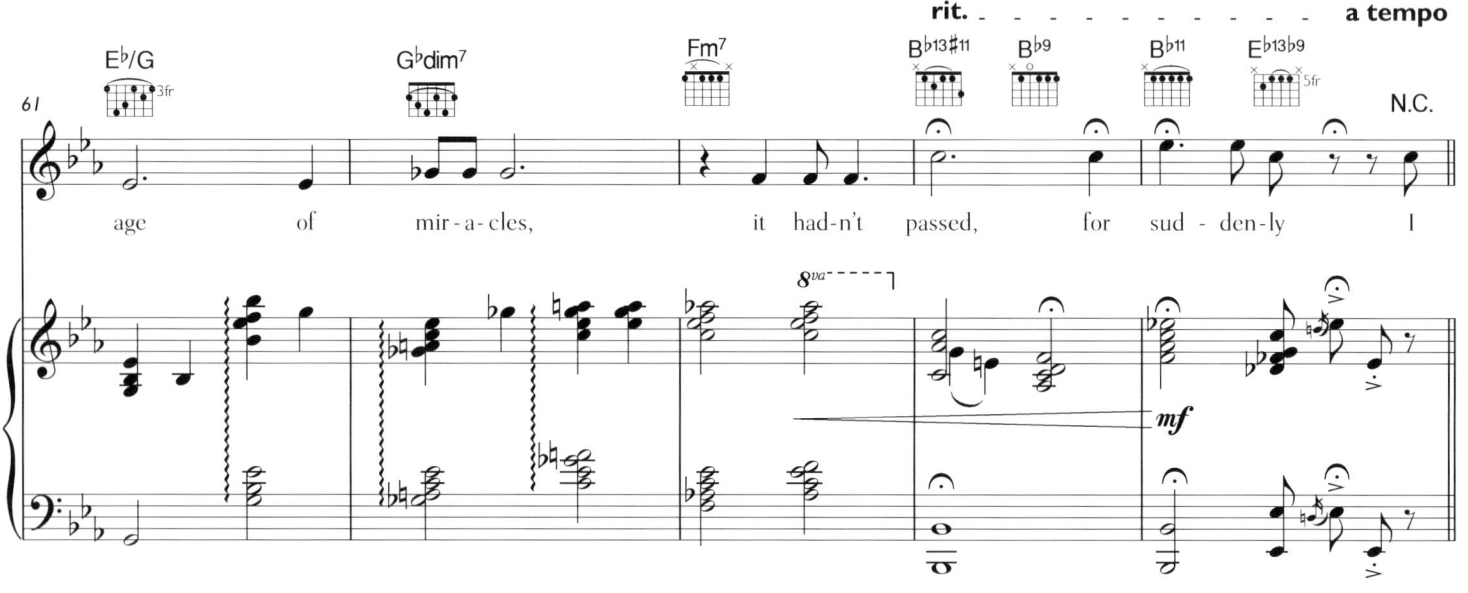
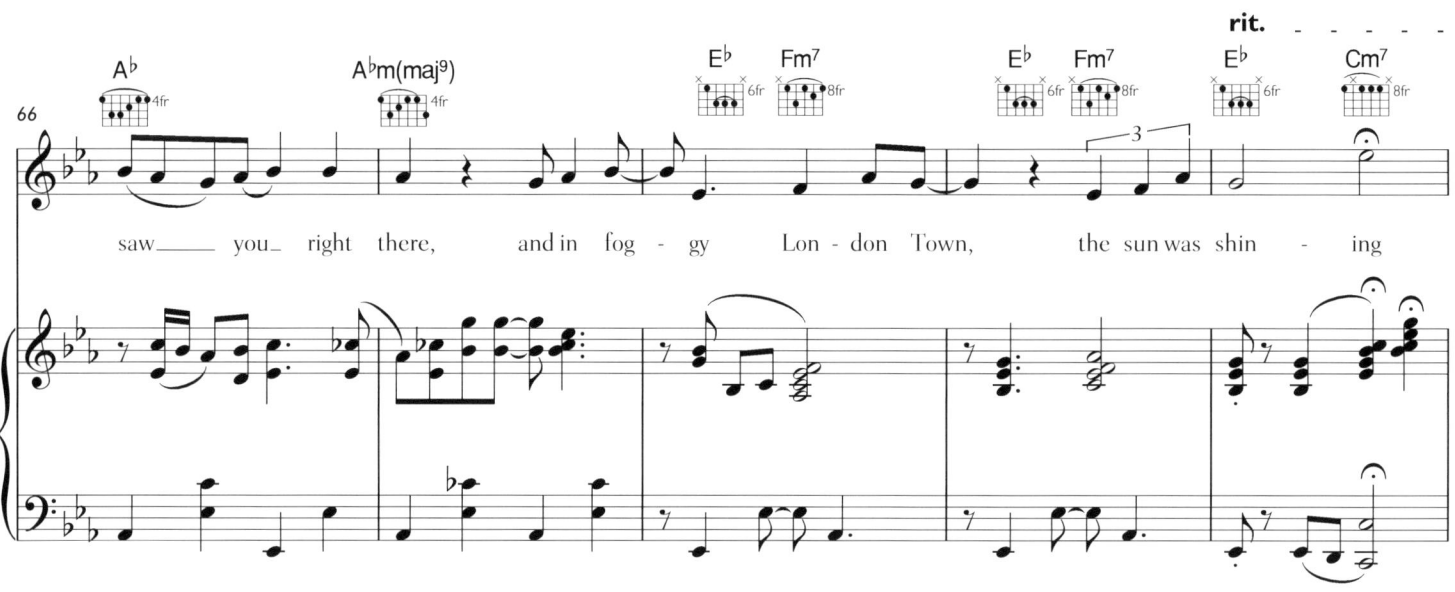

Jamie Cullum

GIVE ME THE SIMPLE LIFE

Words by Harry Ruby
Music by Rube Bloom

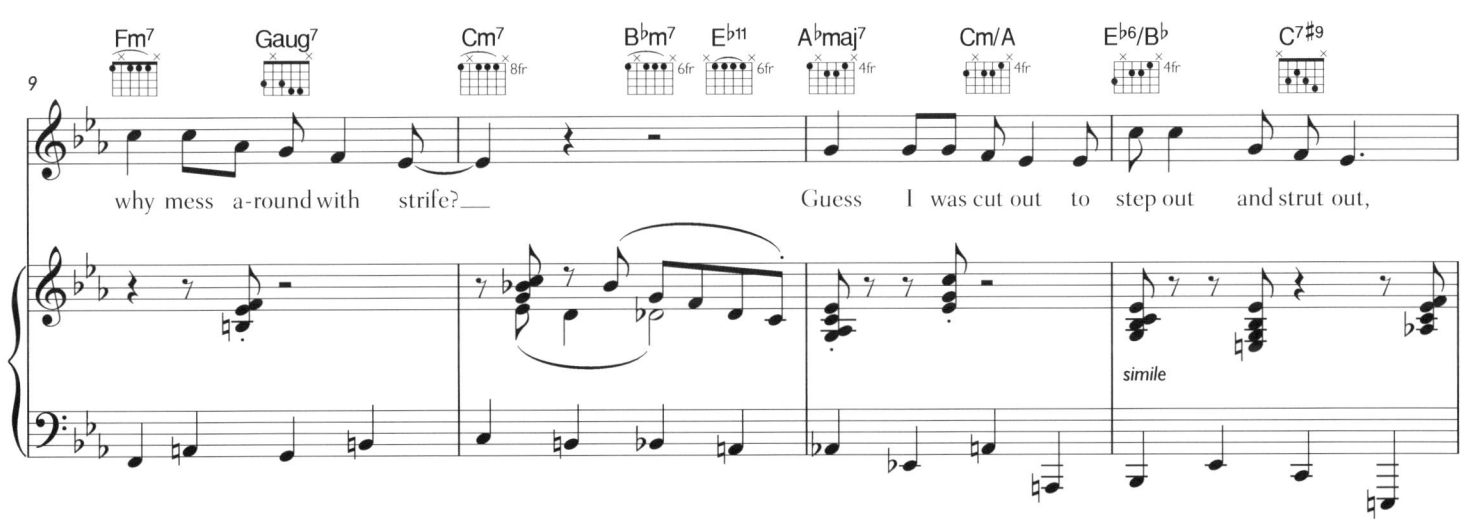

© 1945 (renewed) WB Music Corp
Warner/Chappell Music Ltd

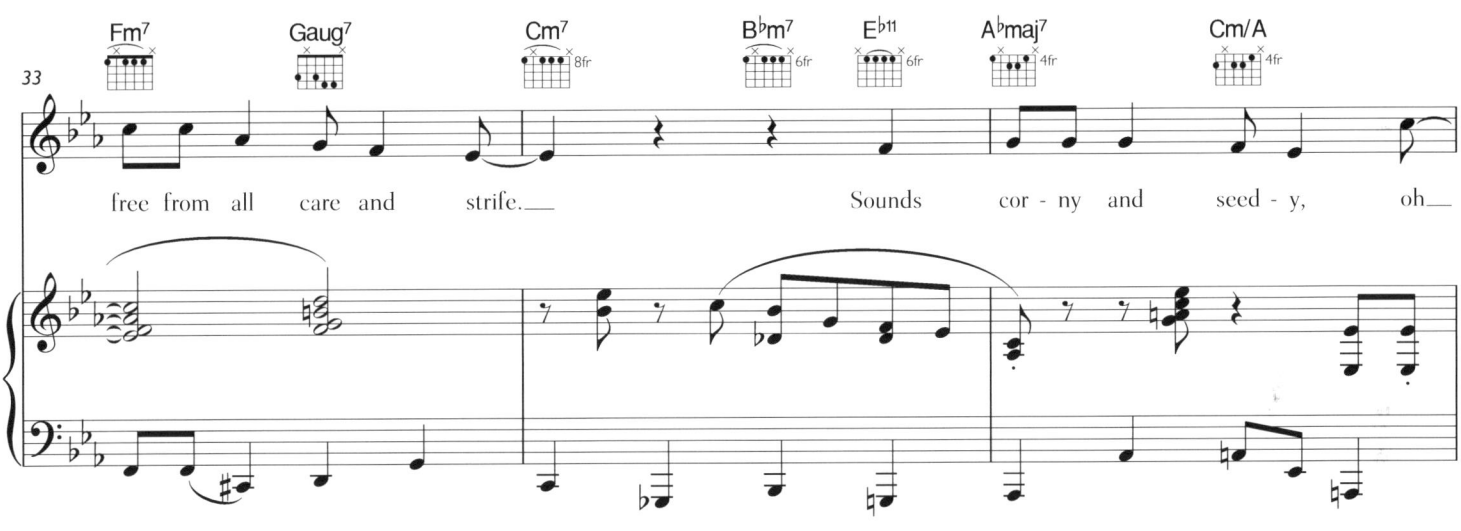
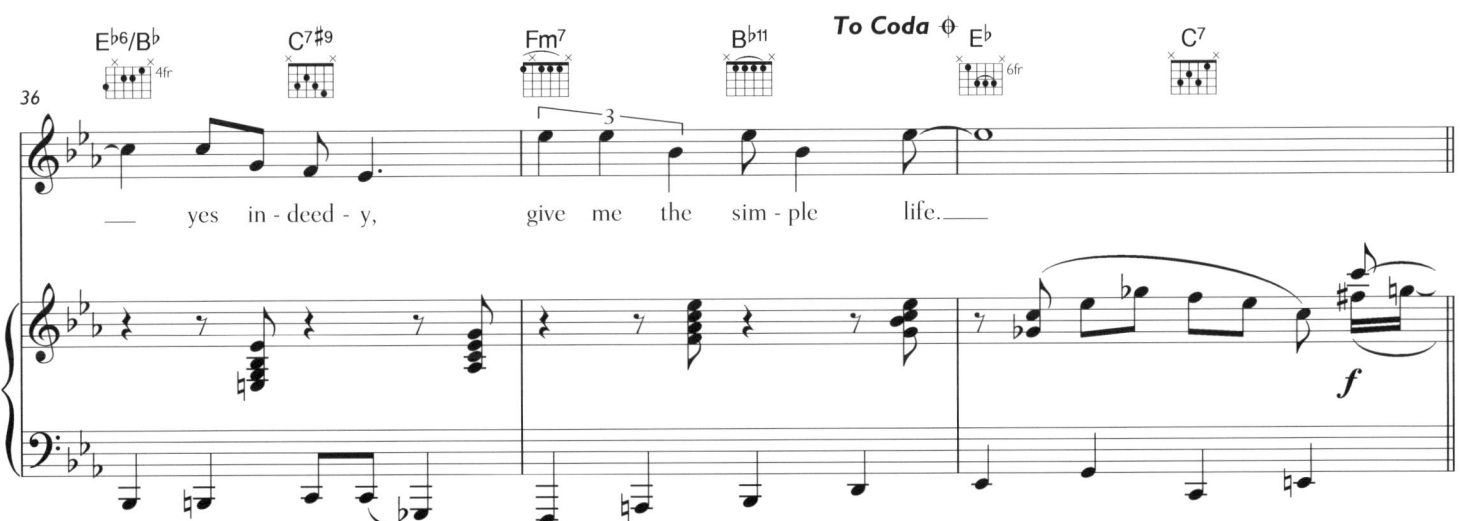

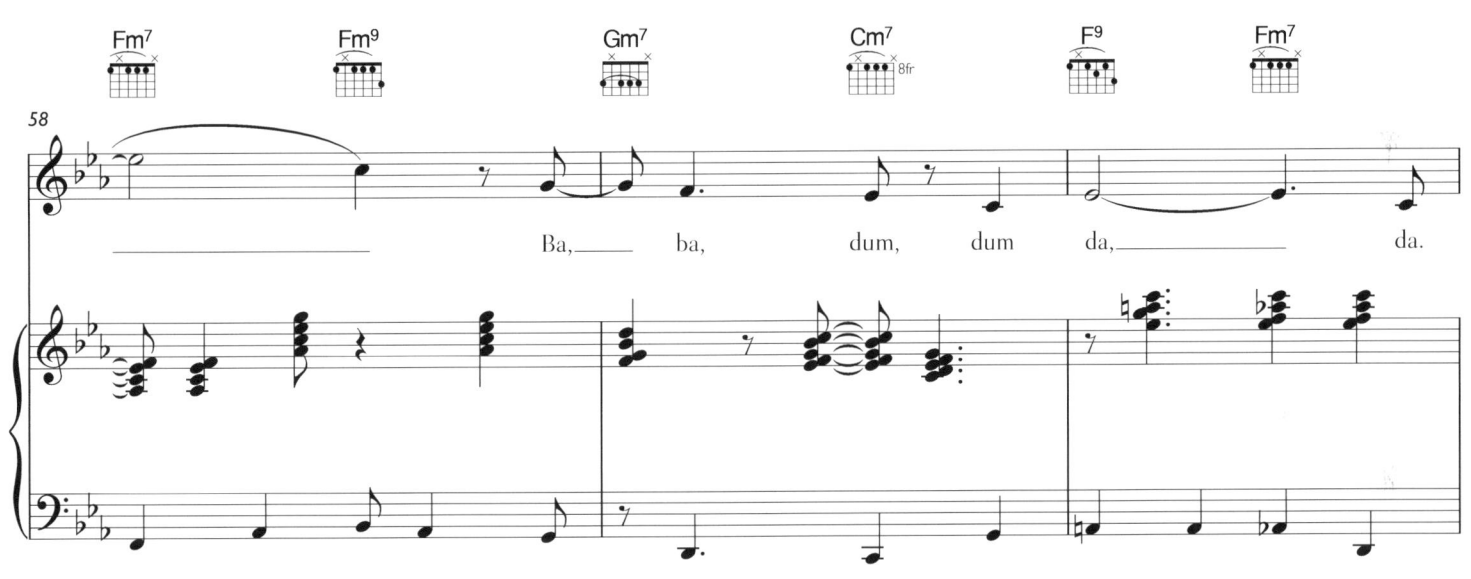

I WISH I KNEW HOW IT WOULD FEEL TO BE FREE

Words and Music by Dick Dallas and Billy Taylor

© 1963 Duane-Music Inc
Westminster Music Ltd

I GET A KICK OUT OF YOU

Words and Music by Cole Porter

© 1934 WB Music Corp
Warner/Chappell North America Ltd

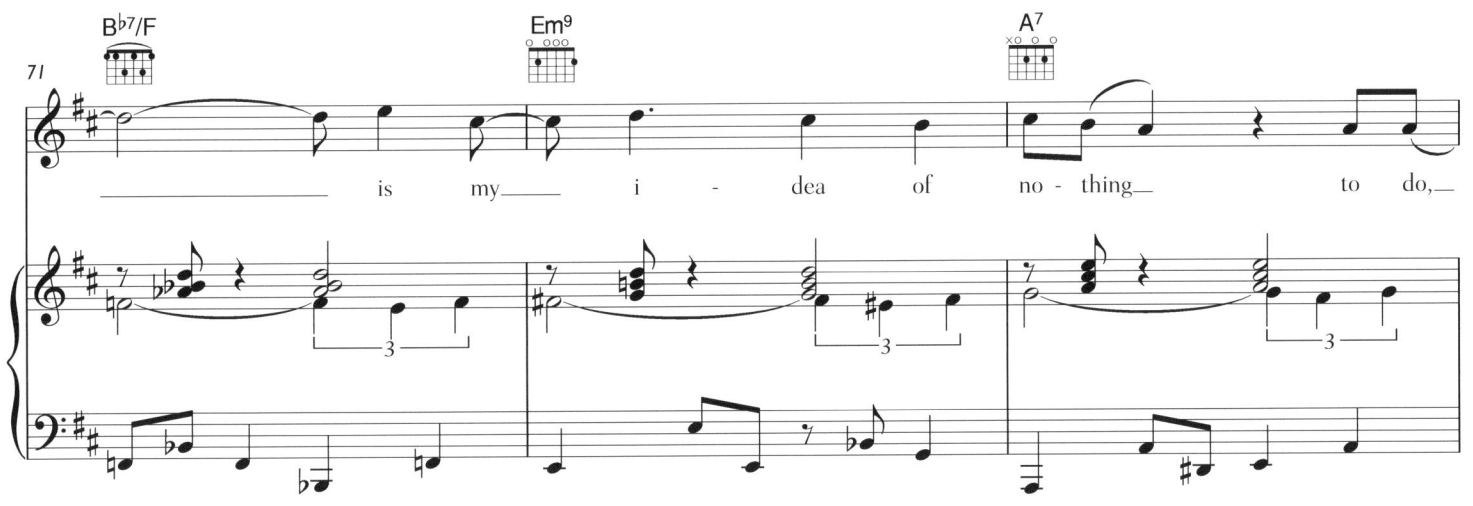
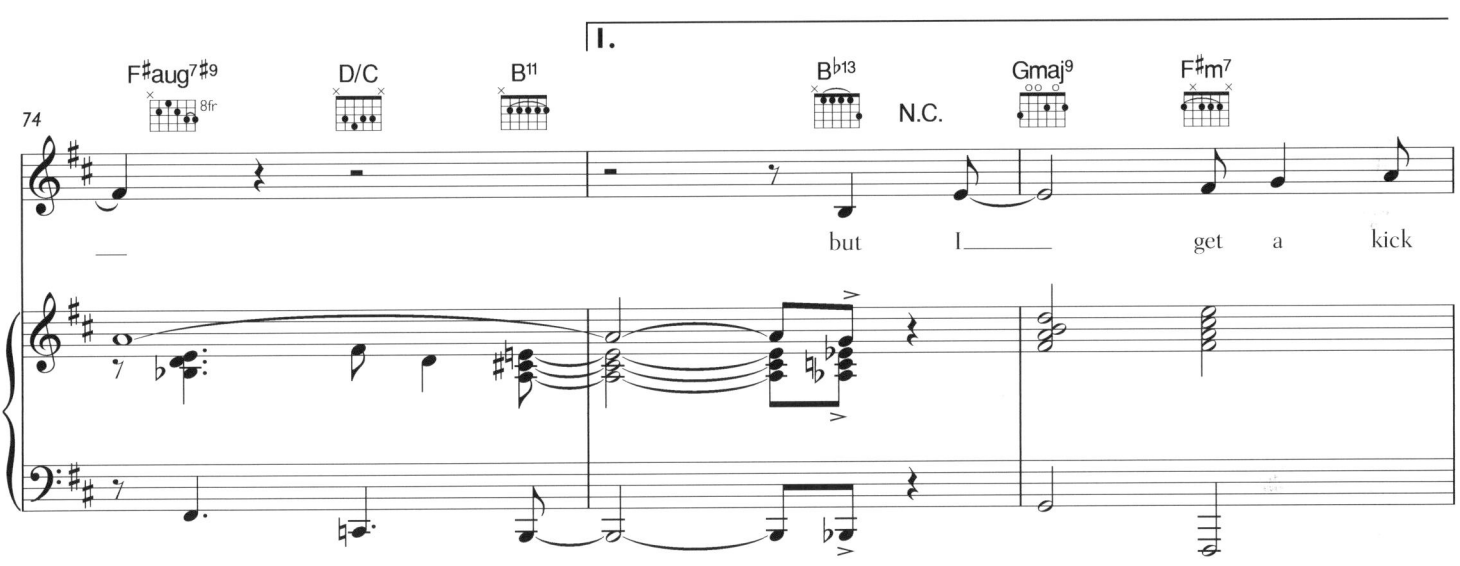
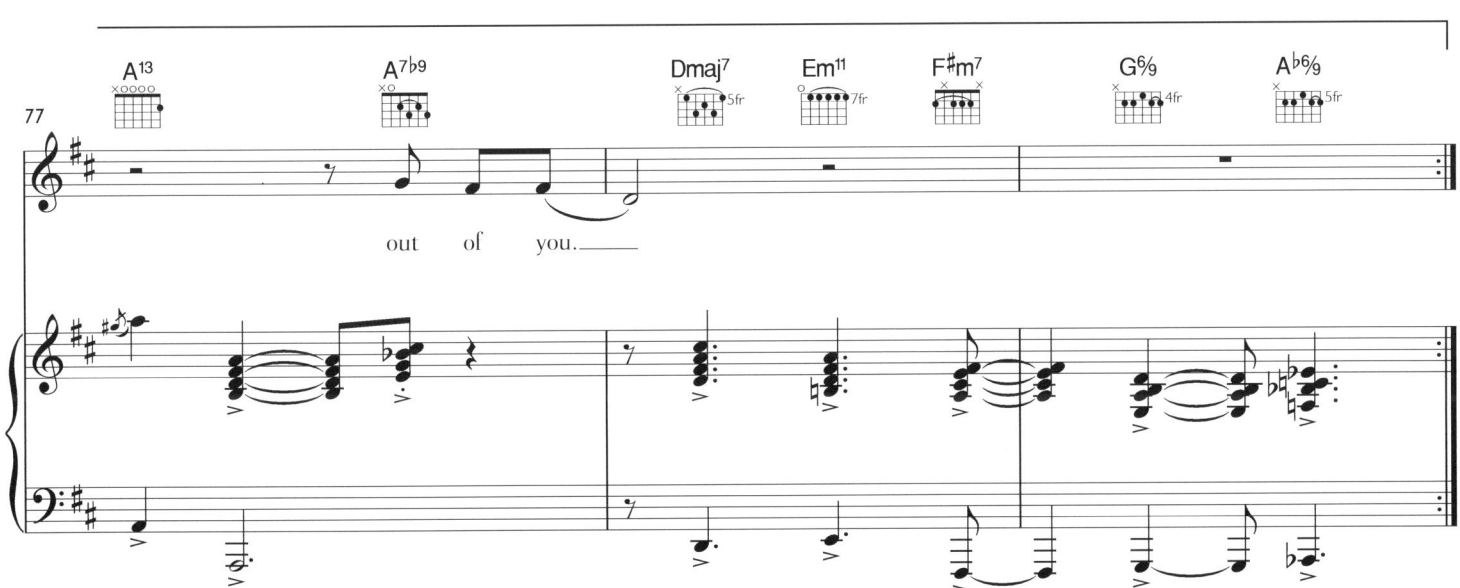

Peggy Lee

I'VE GOT YOU UNDER MY SKIN

Words and Music by Cole Porter

© 1936 Chappell & Co Inc
Warner/Chappell North America Ltd

THE LADY IS A TRAMP

Words by Lorenz Hart
Music by Richard Rodgers

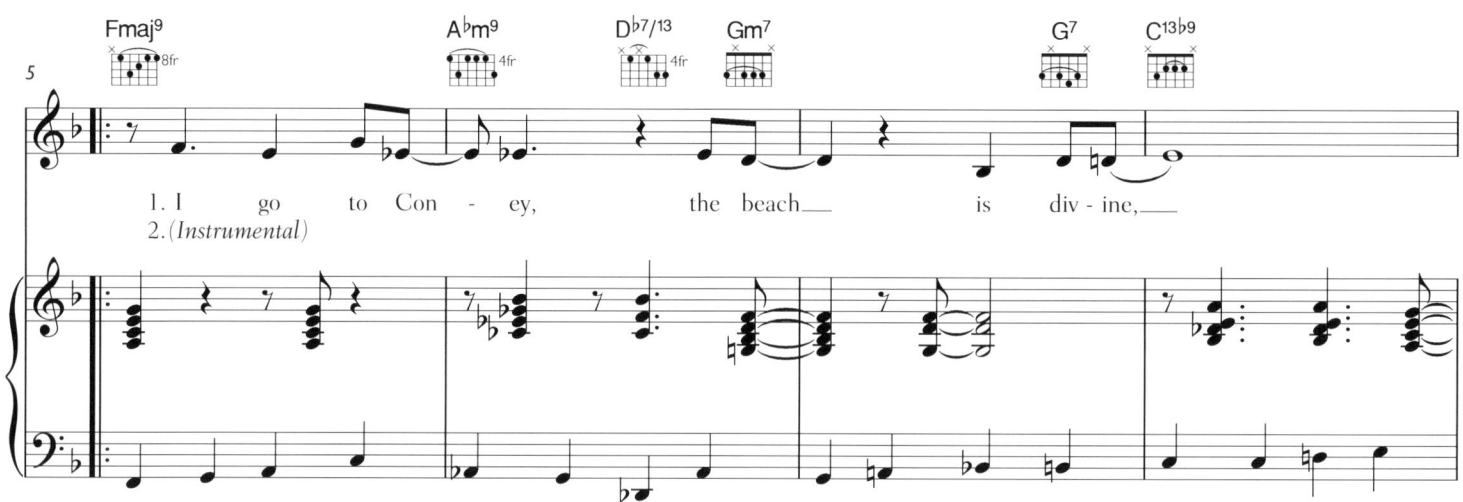

© 1937 Chappell & Co Inc
Warner/Chappell Music Publishing Ltd and
Warner/Chappell North America Ltd

LET THERE BE LOVE

Words by Ian Grant
Music by Lionel Rand

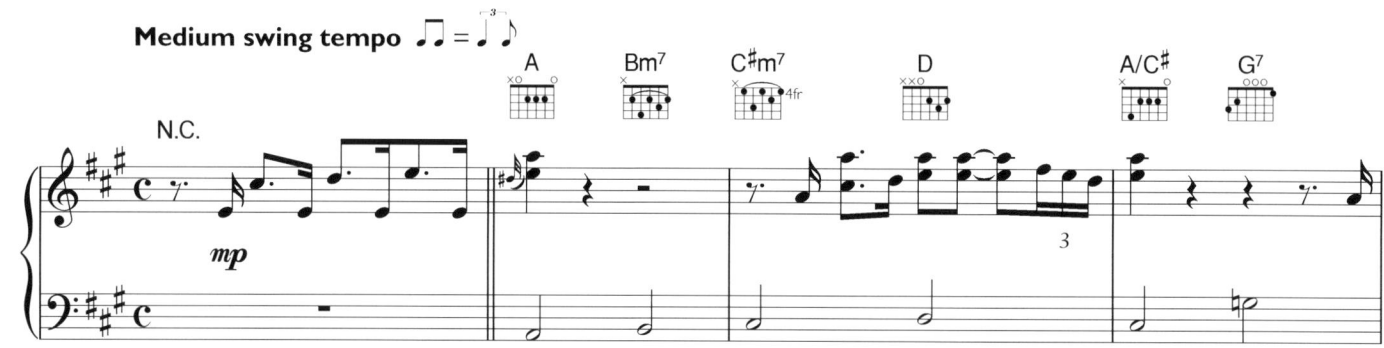
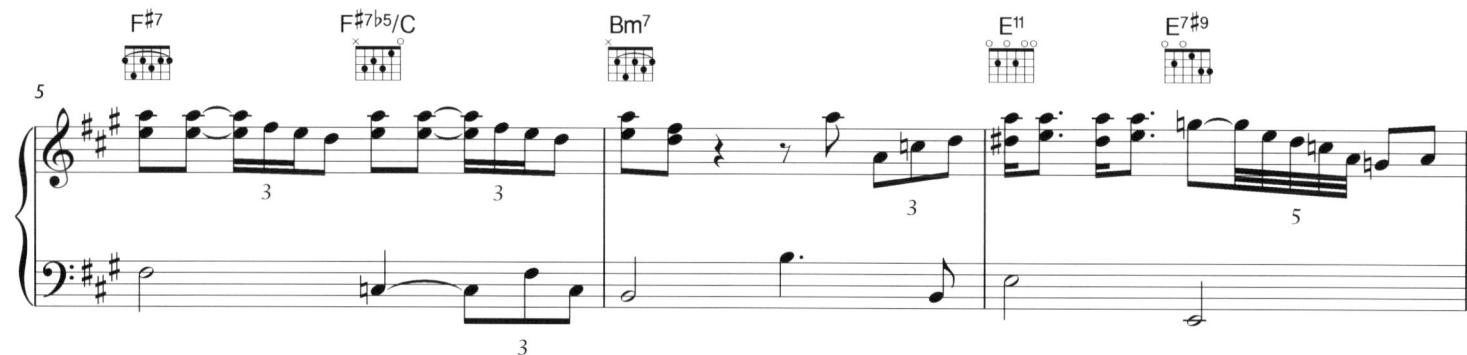
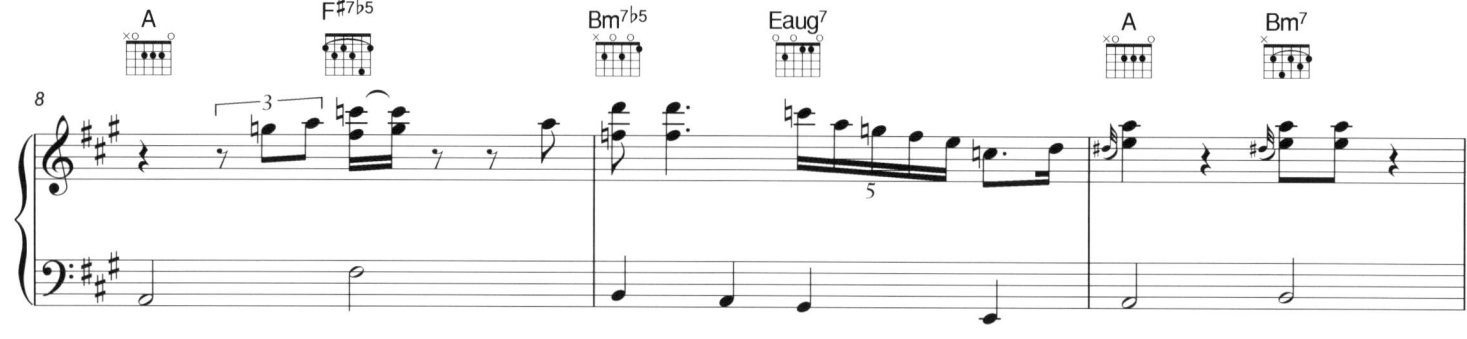

© 1941 Shapiro Bernstein & Co Inc
Warner/Chappell Music Publishing Ltd

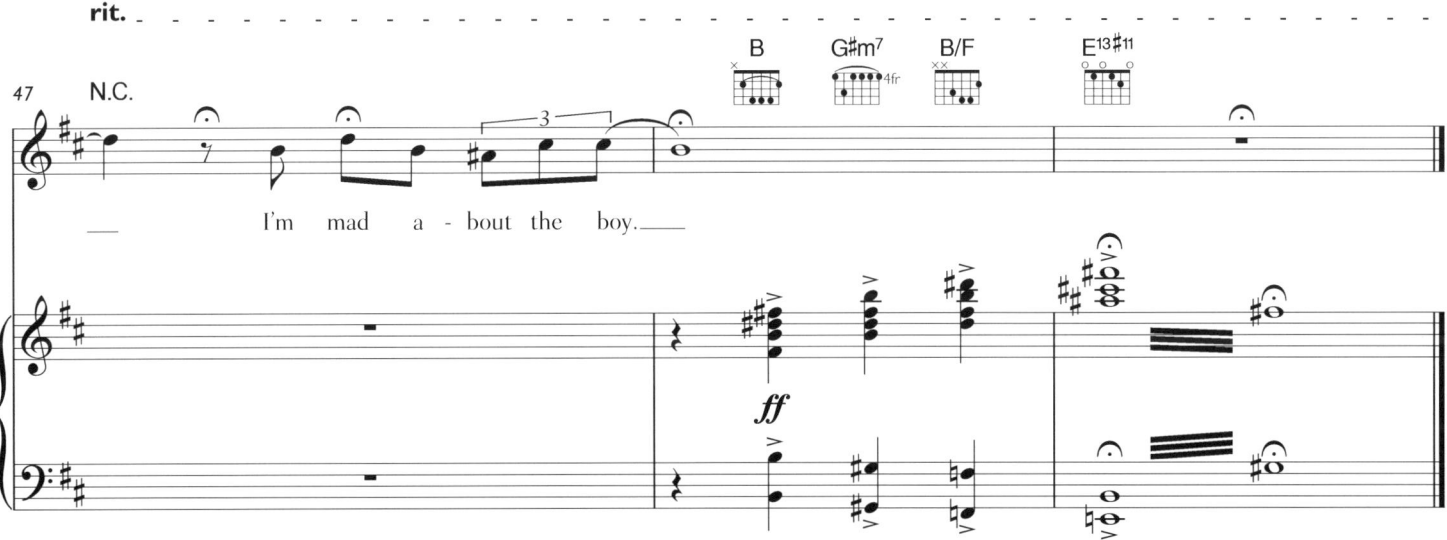

MY FUNNY VALENTINE

Words by Lorenz Hart
Music by Richard Rodgers

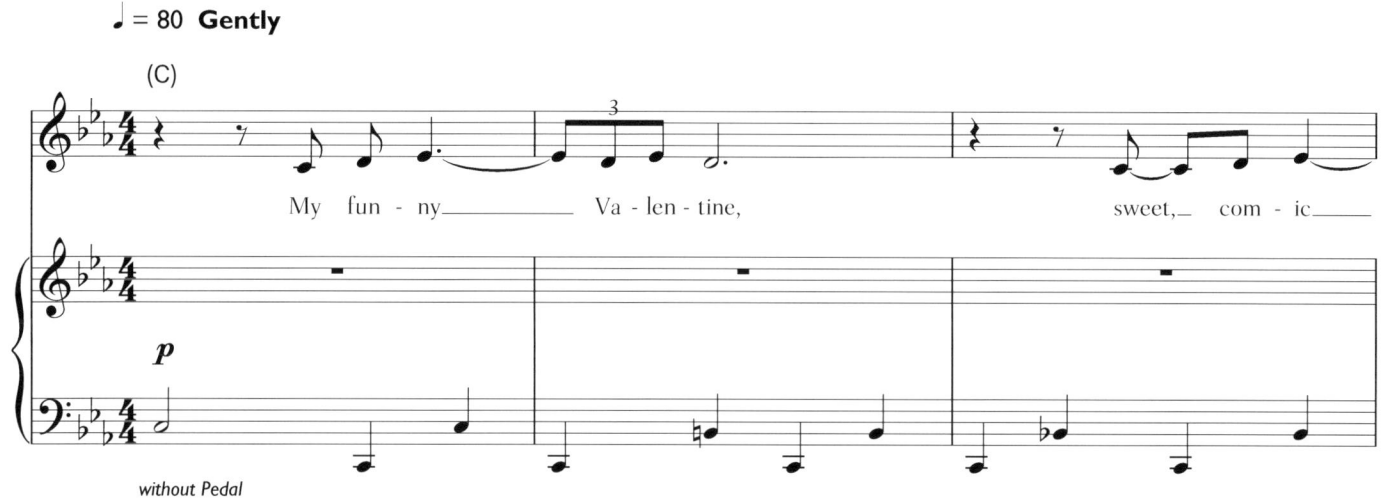
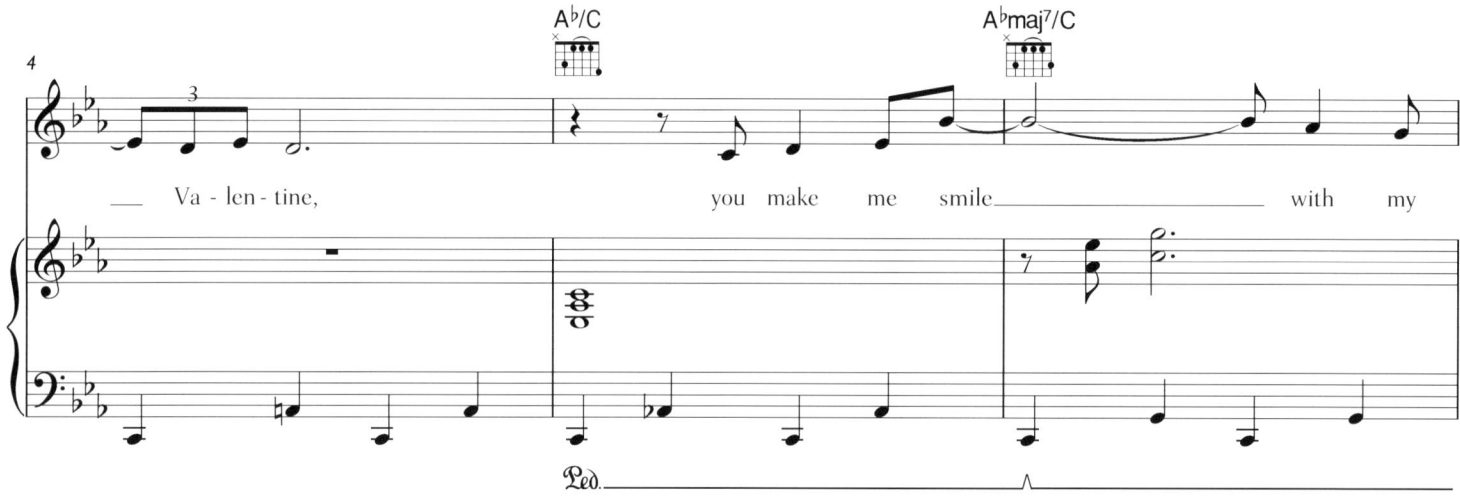
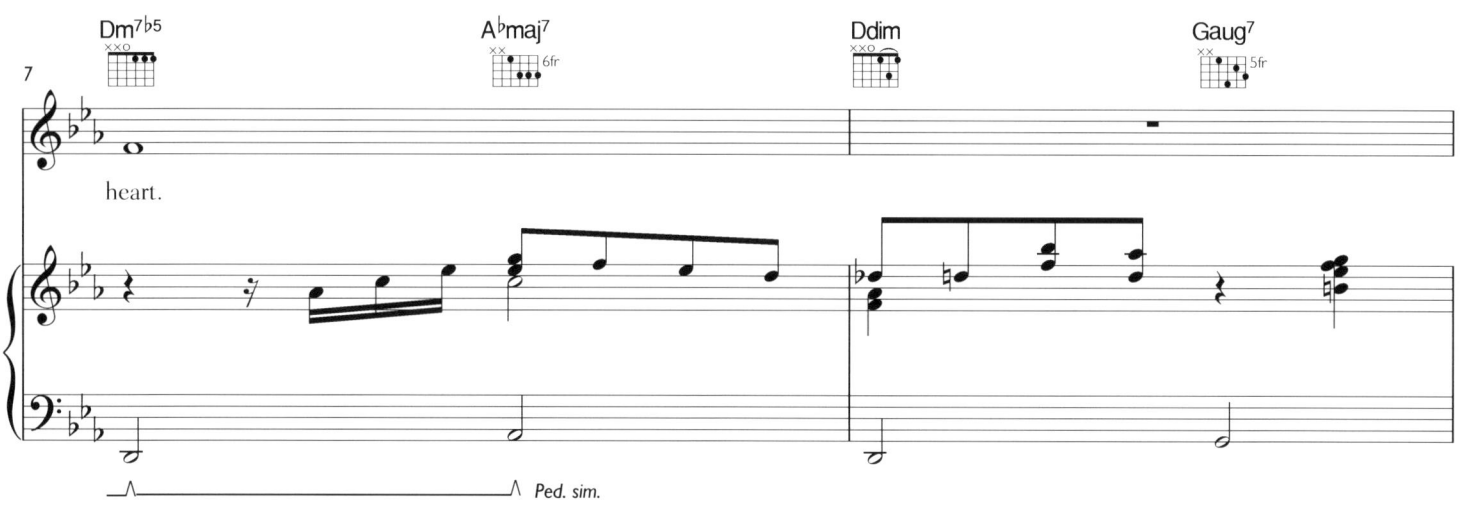

© 1937 Chappell & Co Inc
Warner/Chappell Music Publishing Ltd and
Warner/Chappell North America Ltd

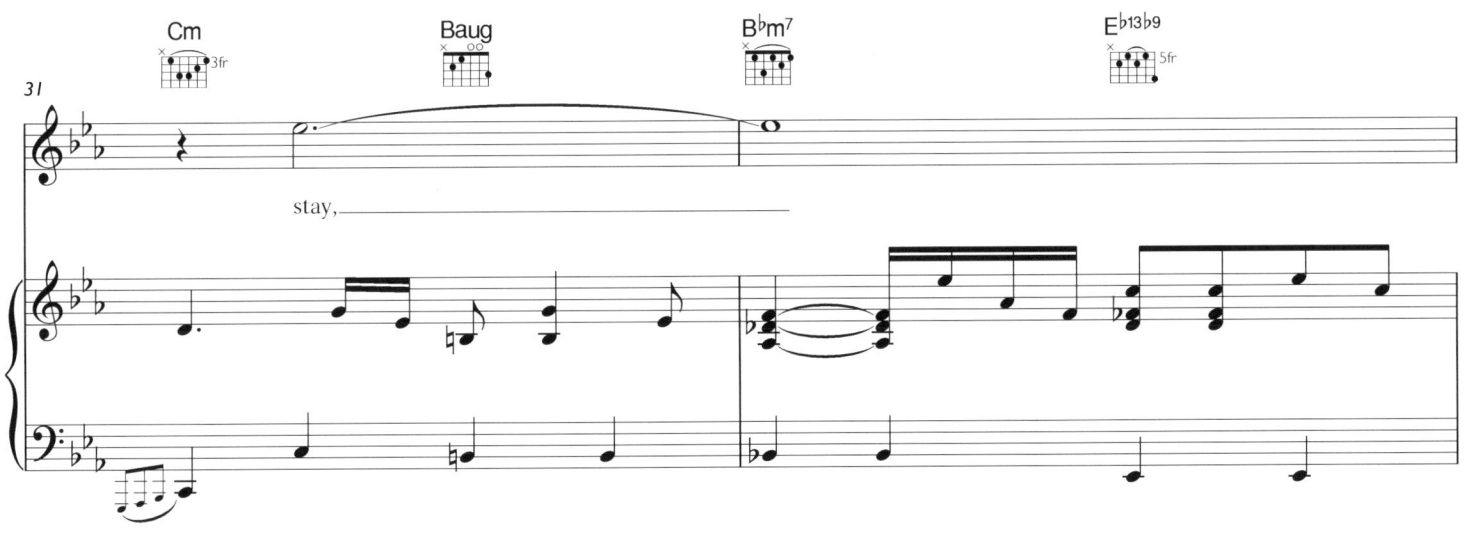

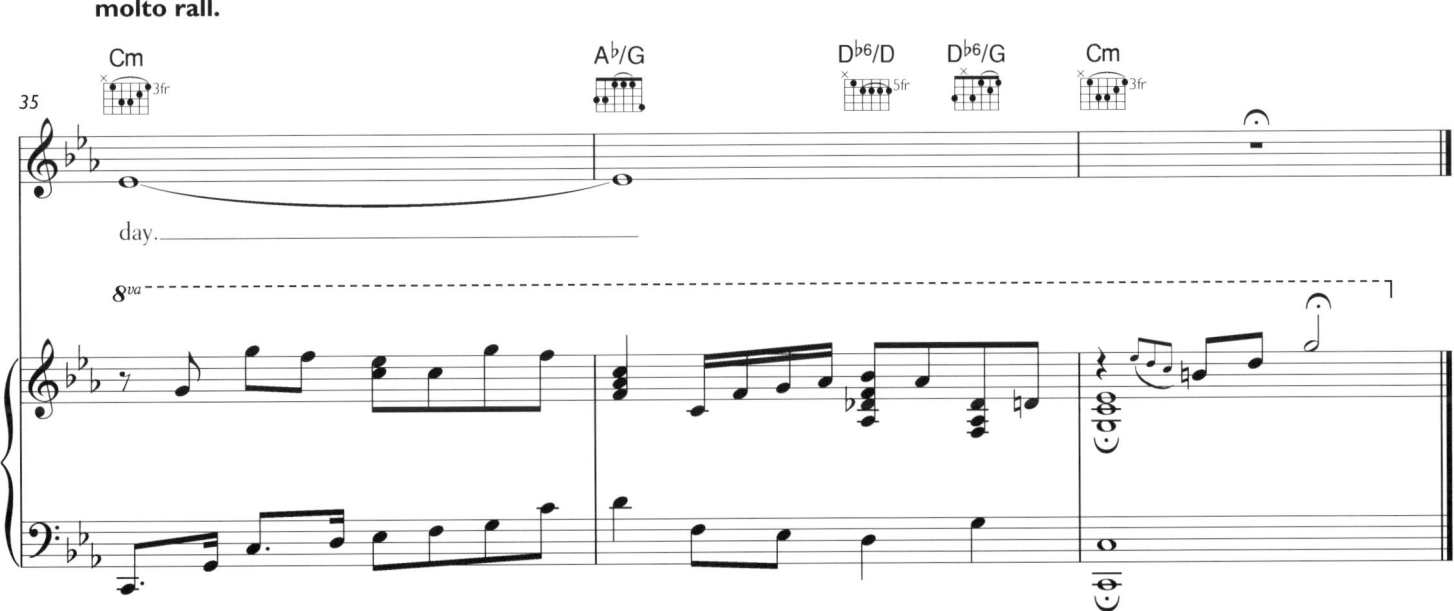

Carmen McRae

'ROUND MIDNIGHT

Words and Music by Cootie Williams,
Bernie Hanighen and Thelonius Monk

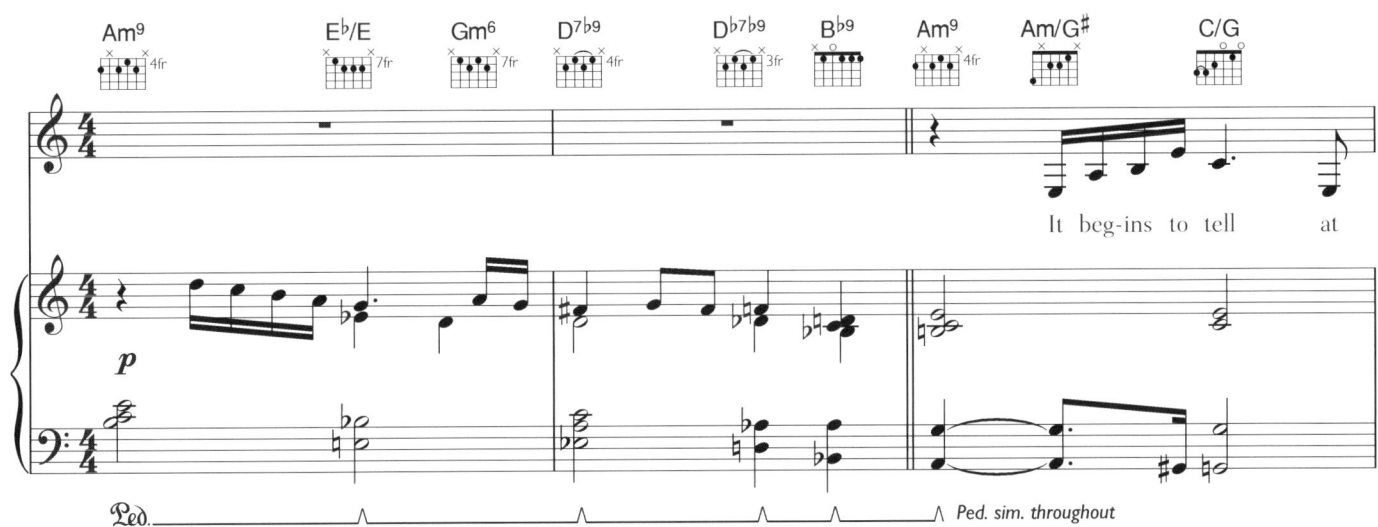

© 1944 (renewed) Advanced Music Corp
Warner/Chappell North America Ltd

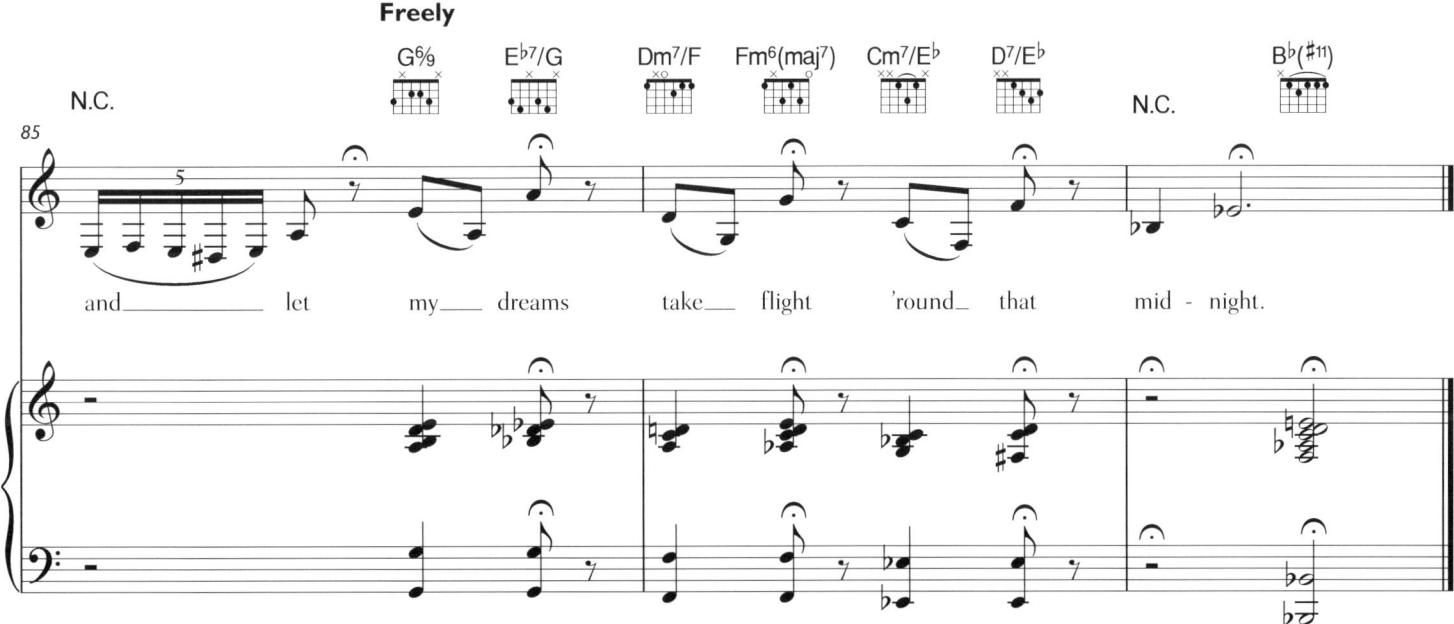

STRANGE FRUIT

Words and Music by Lewis Allen

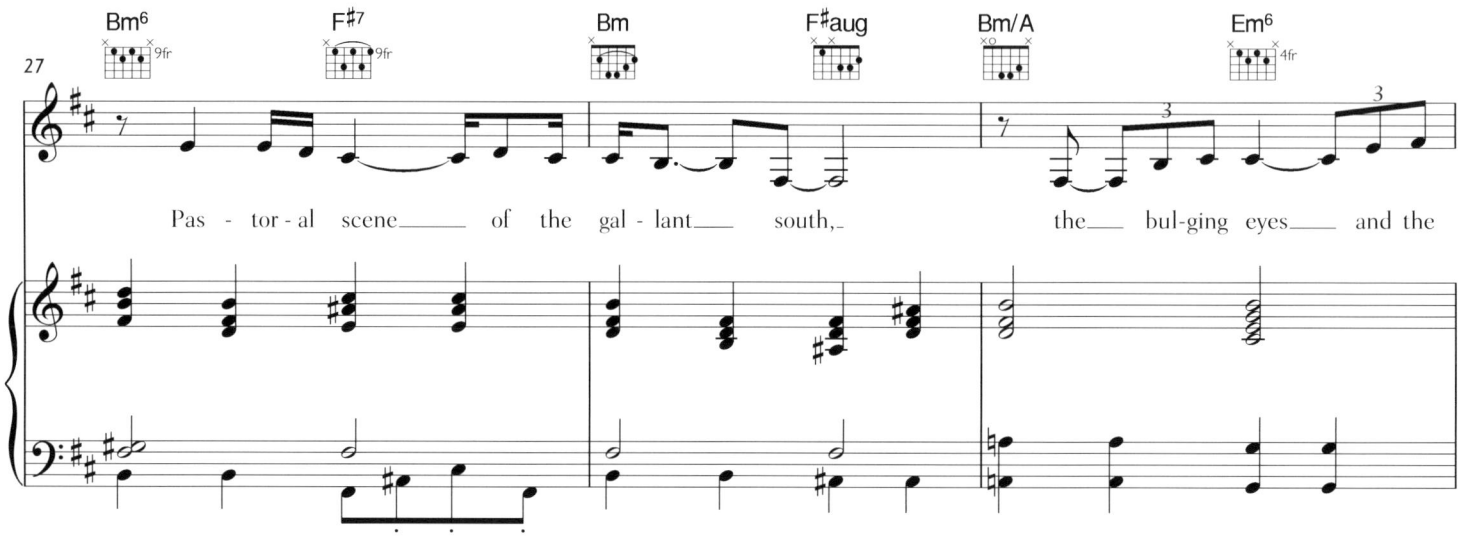
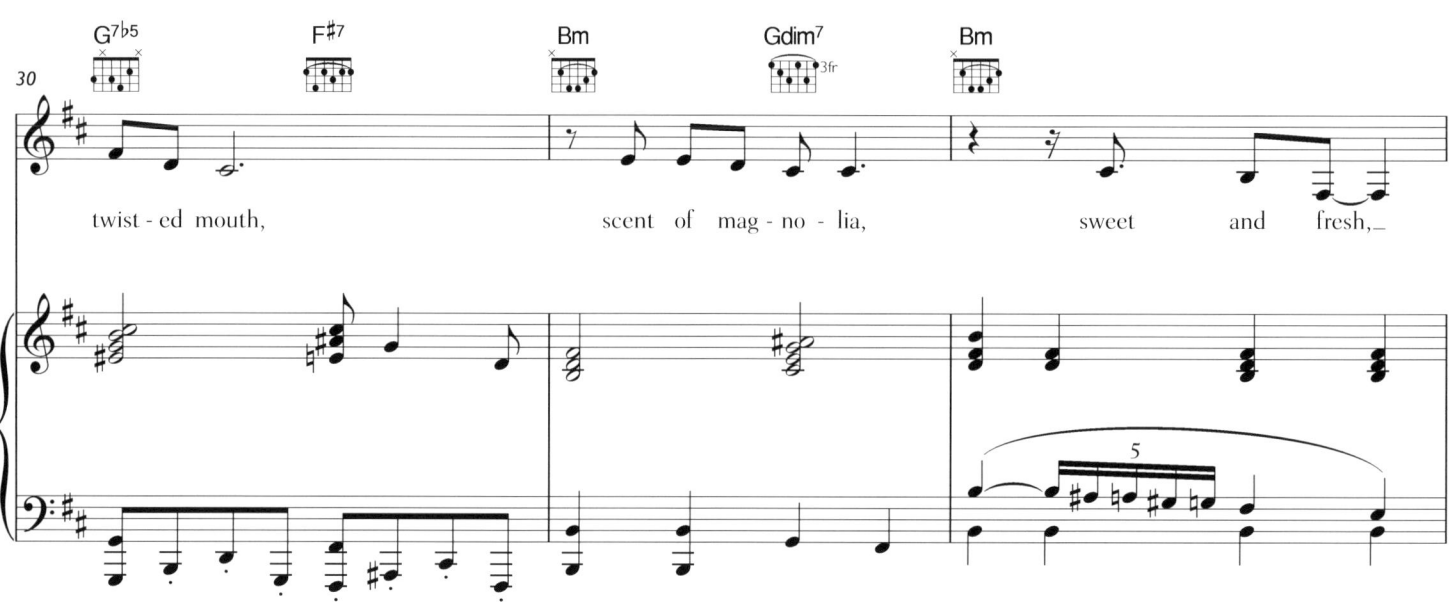

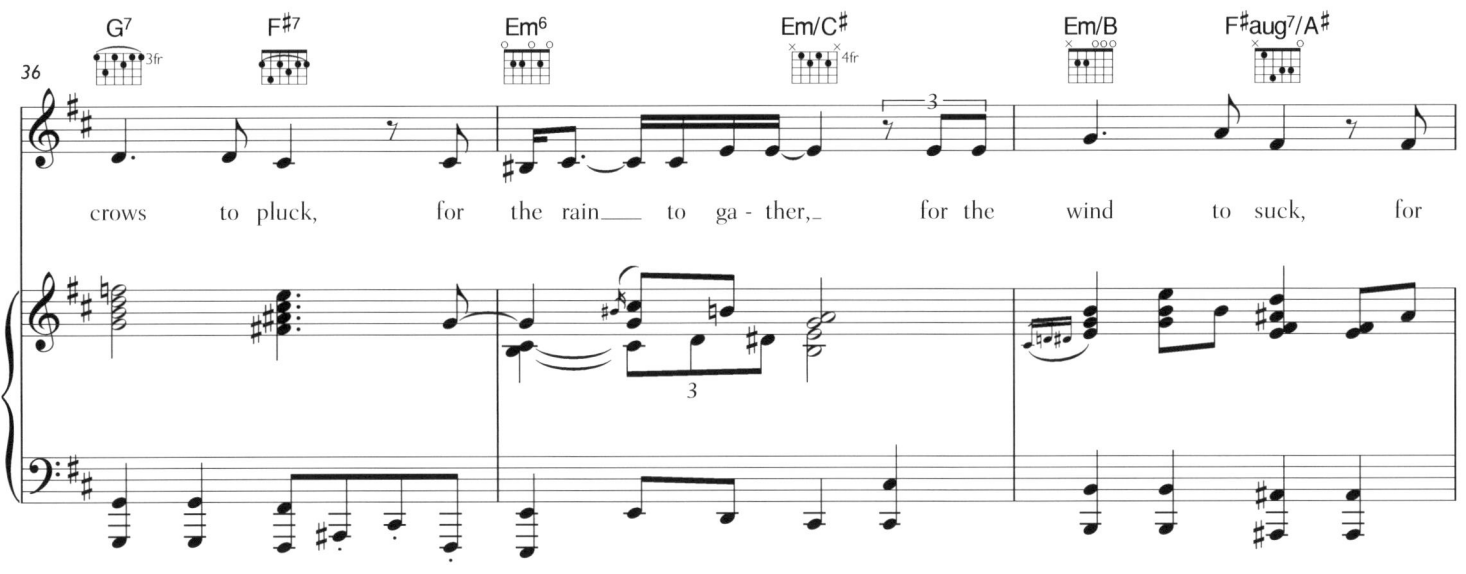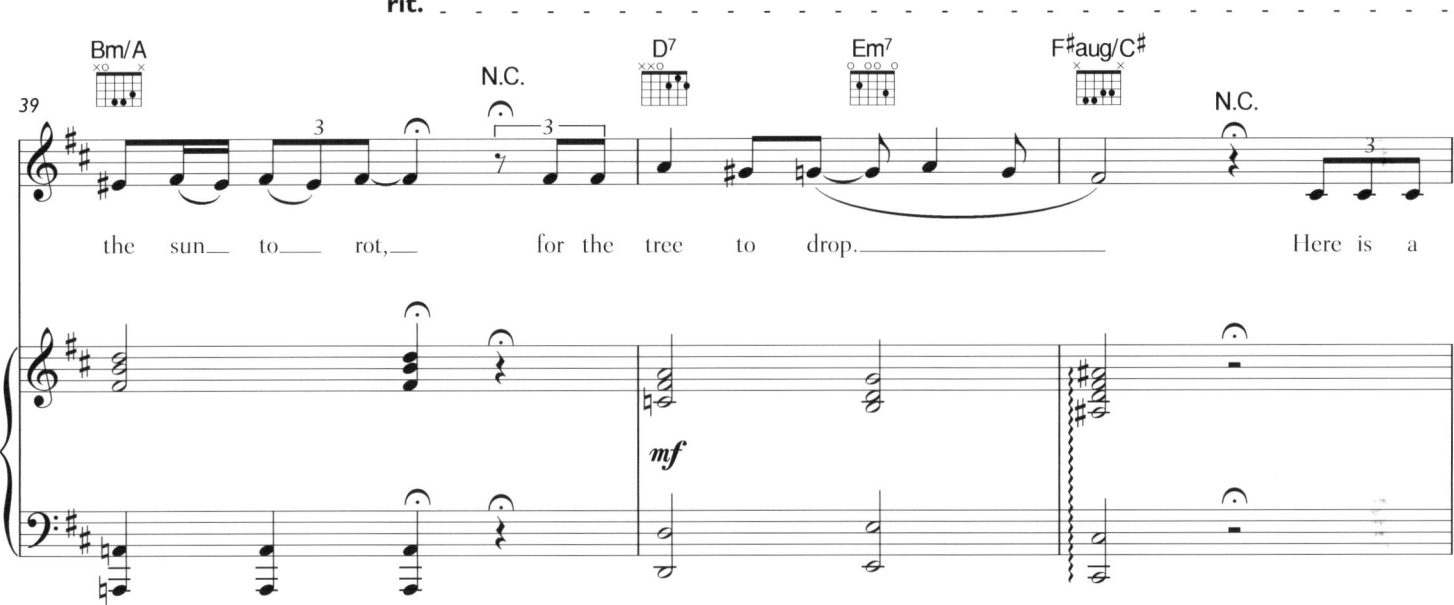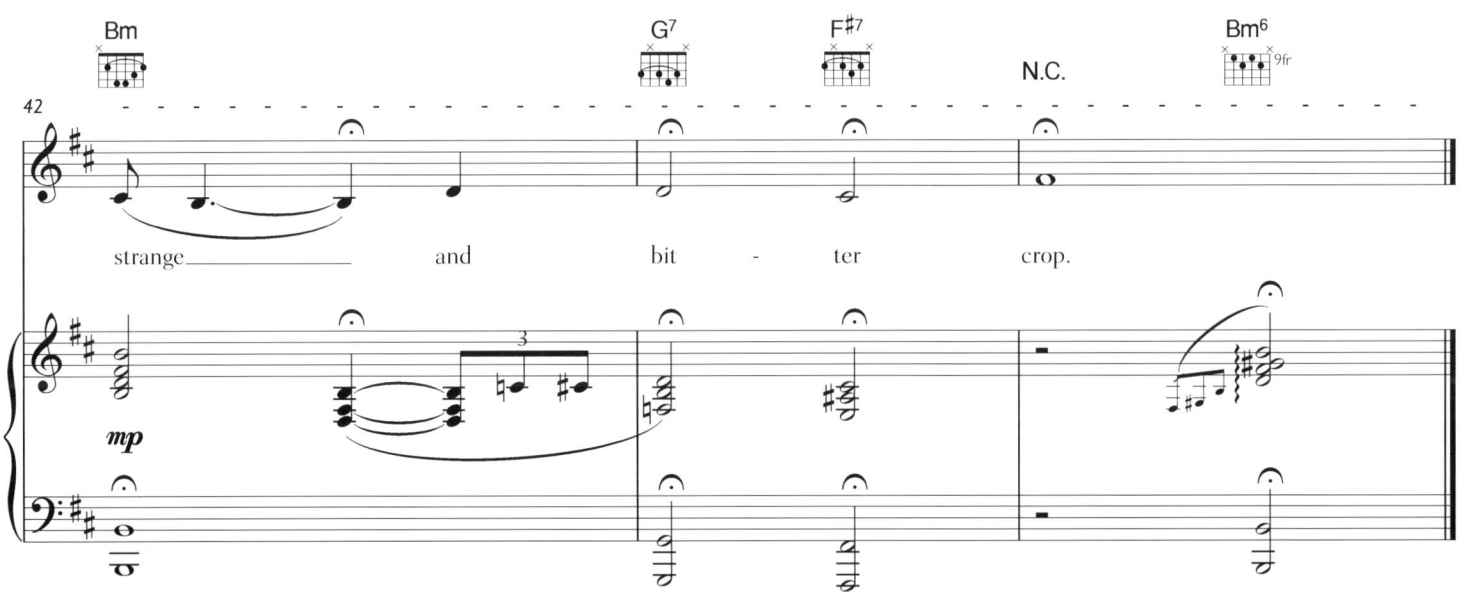

THAT OLD BLACK MAGIC

Words by John Mercer
Music by Harold Arlen

© 1942 Famous Music Corp
Famous Music Publishing Ltd

Sarah Vaughan

WHAT A DIFFERENCE A DAY MADE

Words by Stanley Adams
Music by Maria Grever

© 1934 E. B. Marks Music Corp
Peter Maurice Music Co Ltd

WITCHCRAFT

Words by Carolyn Leigh
Music by Cy Coleman

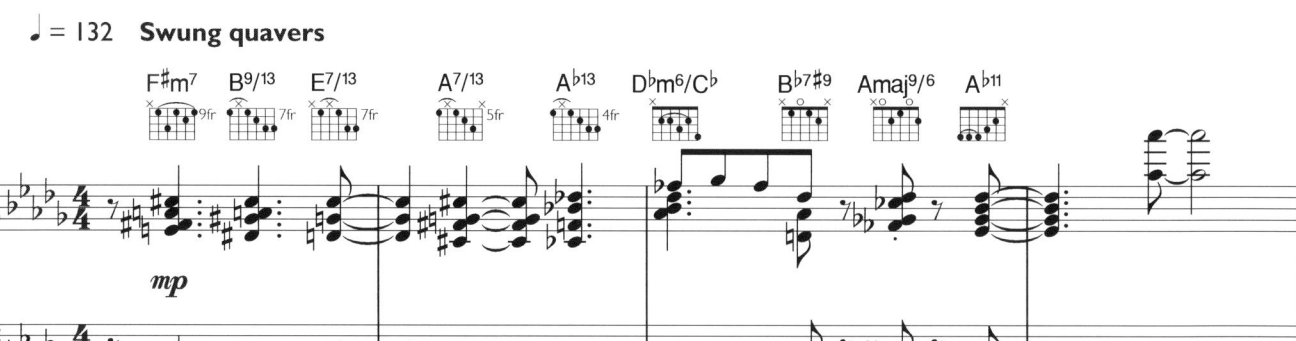
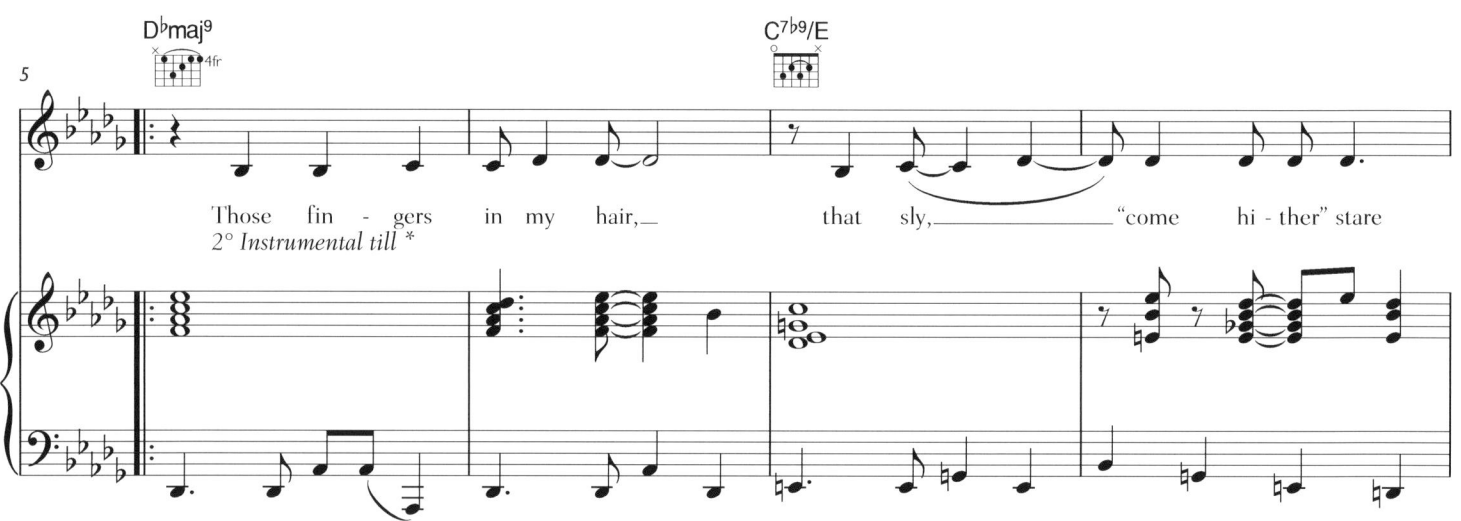

© 1957 Notable Music Co Inc and Morley Music Co Inc
Chappell Morris Ltd and Chrysalis Music Ltd

Nina Simone · The Piano Songbook

Nina Simone Piano Songbook Vol.1 (PVG)
ISBN: 0-571-52863-5

Ain't Got No, I Got Life
Don't Let Me Be Misunderstood
Feeling Good
I Loves You Porgy
I Put A Spell On You
I Think It's Going To Rain Today
I Want A Little Sugar In My Bowl
I Wish I Knew How It Would Feel To Be Free
The Look Of Love
Mr. Bojangles
My Baby Just Cares For Me
Nobody's Fault But Mine
Since I Fell For You
Sinnerman
To Be Young, Gifted and Black

To buy Faber Music publications or to find out about the full range of titles available
please contact your local music retailer or Faber Music sales enquiries:

Faber Music Ltd, Burnt Mill, Elizabeth Way, Harlow CM20 2HX
Tel: +44 (0) 1279 82 89 82   Fax: +44 (0) 1279 82 89 83
sales@fabermusic.com   fabermusic.com